Bugs in a Dump

Written by Shayla Wilson

Illustrated by Rob Dvorak

AF411744

Word Families: Short *u*

bugs	mug
dump	jump
run	fun

High-Frequency Words

blue	going	how	live	they
funny	have	know	play	three

1

Three funny bugs live in a dump.

Three funny bugs are going to play.

They jump in a blue mug.

They run up a pile of dimes.

The funny bugs are going to hide.

Do you see the bugs?

The bugs know how to have fun!